ACTING FOR DANCERS™

ACTING FOR DANCERS™

Dancing with Intention,
How to be a Dance Storyteller

J. Alex Brinson

with

Sarah Brinson

U Publishing, GB Group (US) LLC

GB Group Creative Inc.
1800, 401 West Georgia Street
Vancouver, BC V6B 5A1,
Canada

Photography by Beth Laird
Additional Photo Images by Nigel Edwards
Book Design by Jenna Oakley

Inquiries: info@gobrinson.com

ISBN-10:0990630102
ISBN-13:978-0-9906301-0-4

1. Dance 2. Theatre   3. Arts & Entertainment   4. Education

Printed in the USA

This book is dedicated to all of the amazing and very brave dancers around the world that helped us develop *Acting for Dancers*™.

CONTENTS

A NOTE FROM THE AUTHORS

As far as we've been able to determine, the concepts presented here constitute an entirely new method that will help dancers prepare themselves to give the best performances possible. Intuitive, logical, and absolutely brilliant, this book simplifies the concepts and keys that can unlock the dancer's ability to become a true storyteller, allowing the effective performer to truly engage the audience.

A quick, simple read, it's loaded with advanced theory. I advise you to take the time to read it over and over and over again. I encourage you to study these concepts and really try to integrate them into your process. You will enjoy dancing more than you ever have before, and people *will* notice.

- J. and Sarah Brinson

INTRODUCTION

A child's imagination is vivid, sharp, and powerful. The tools that we explore herein will ignite that imaginative fire, connecting it to the dancer's instrument and the choreographer's movement to make powerful, beautiful, full, and purposeful engaged dancing, or "dance storytelling."

Equipping the next generation of dance artists with tools for their artistic development, we are delighted to help all dancers – from young students to aspiring professionals – become the future educated and proficient theatre collaborators who will be a choreographer's first choice.

Dancing is more fun when your imagination is engaged, and when you feel connected to a specific story, purpose, or circumstance, and when you've rehearsed and learned the movement well enough to let it all go – when you're feeling just free to dance!

Your insecurities about the moves, your body, or what viewers are thinking all fall away as you explore a character and take a journey utilizing your own very powerful imagination.

Acting for Dancers is a combination of techniques, methods, and games based on learning that comes from years of our study in the theatre with theatre artists including Moni and Mina Yakim, Frank Deal, Jane Nichols, Richard Feldman, Carolyn Serota, and many more.

CHAPTER I

FOCUS, CONCENTRATION, AND RELAXATION

My mother-in-law is a professional golfer and often connects the success of a golfer's putting (the "short game") with the ability to visualize the ball dropping into the hole. Before a shot is initiated, the golfer will envision the ball coming off the putter head and arcing across the green to smoothly drop into the hole.

This can work for dancers, too. In order to be successful, whether a golfer or a dance storyteller, you must have a clear mind, open and ready to receive the vision and instruction of your body instrument; this requires focused and concentrated thinking.

Have you ever considered these questions: "What does the painter paint with: his hands or his brain?" "Does a dancer dance with her body or her brain?"

The answer isn't just one or the other, of course. Using your body is essential, of course – and the engagement of the imagination is a process that takes place in the mind. This "mind" is equivalent to a muscle that should be worked, developed, toned, and strengthened for agility.

Just as you take ballet class daily to strengthen your turnout, articulate through your body, and develop physical strength, the same is required of your focus, concentration, and relaxation. We cannot urge you enough to embrace the importance of taking the time to develop all of these processes.

At the foundation of our process we lay "focus and concentration," the tool that needs to be in every dancer's toolbox.

Through games, exercises, and practice, we dancers strengthen our ability to clear our minds, enabling us to focus strictly on one thing at any given moment. For most of us, that's not an easy thing to do; however, to be open and available for the story to come through your body and emotions it must pass easily through the mind. If the mind is not clear, the instrument will be inhibited from responding organically to what it's receiving. We'll speak about this more in the next chapter, "Listening with the Entire Body."

Tension, whether in your body or your mind, is the greatest enemy to this foundational tool. Strain, stress, and anxiety all constitute tension, and a mind that is affected by stress or tension cannot think as clearly as it should. Tension is no friend to the artist.

Often in workshop class settings, the dancers who are the most relaxed are crowned as the most interesting to watch. You've probably had the experience, as an audience member watching a "tight" artist, of becoming tight and nervous yourself; you're almost sometimes scared for such dancers while they perform.

To clarify a question that's often been raised: being free of tension and full of relaxation does not mean that you cannot be dynamic in movement; what it does mean, though, is that your approach is free and open, and not rigid or riddled with habitual choices. When you are full of listening and can respond organically to what is going on in and around you – that's when you'll be dancing at your best.

It's no fun watching tension, and if you need

proof, remember that the best actors and dancers (along with the best athletes, doctors, lawyers, and even engineers) are often referred to as being effortless, cool, calm and "so natural." This comes from working in a way that's relaxed, focused, and concentrated.

If you don't yet have a method to work on your focus, concentration, and relaxation, you should invest in some kind of training to develop your process. It's during workshop exercises and in real theatrical settings that the most focused and concentrated dance artist does some of the greatest work.

How can you apply what you've learned
in Chapter 1 to increase your level of focus,
concentration and relaxation while you dance?

_____

_____

_____

_____

_____

_____

_____

_____

_____

_____

_____

_____

_____

_____

_____

_____

_____

_____

_____

_____

_____

_____

_____

_____

Notes: _____

_____

_____

_____

_____

_____

_____

_____

_____

_____

_____

_____

_____

_____

_____

_____

_____

_____

_____

_____

_____

_____

_____

_____

_____

_____

_____

_____

_____

_____

_____

_____

CHAPTER 2

LISTENING WITH
THE ENTIRE BODY

There have been times when your mom, sister, brother, wife, husband, or friend gives you "that look" without saying anything – but you know exactly what they mean! What is happening in that moment... how is it that you understand what they're communicating to you, when they're not using any words?

In dance storytelling, your body tells the story and your imagination, when free, should envelop and engage your whole or entire body, from your little toe to the last hair on the top of your head.

Dancers are naturally great actors because of how well they know and understand their bodies. As a dancer, you are very familiar with articulating movement with your body without the use of words or any other kind of oral communication.

Actors initially have a better understanding of using their imagination to paint thought-pictures, but once a dancer grasps the fundamentals of these methods, they normally integrate very quickly because of how well they know and understand their bodies.

This may seem like a puzzle, but it's really very straightforward. Consider this: Acting entails "reacting." Bad acting is just "acting." Bad acting seems unreal and unbelievable; on the other hand, great acting doesn't seem like acting at all! Now, the question is how we as dancers can achieve great acting within our dance.

By listening! It's that simple. If you listen, and listen with your entire body, you will no longer have to act, as you can simply react. The bad-acting trap can overwhelm you when you don't have the answer and you're just faking it! Good acting means no faking; faking is the sign of a lazy or untrained artist who doesn't take the time to prepare.

During our workshop weekends we do extensive work to strengthen our listening ability. Many young artists think that listening is the same as just hearing the music and making sure they're moving within tempo. Yes, hearing the music is part of listening – but only a small part. If we go back to the image of Mom giving us "that look" – what part of our body are we listening with, what part is Mom speaking with, if not verbally?

Our bodies and brains are very powerful, but as you probably know, we only use a fraction of their abilities. We as artists have one of the greatest gifts, and that's the ability to use additional parts of our brain and its amazing power, and deliver meaning with our bodies. Listening with your entire body means using more of your nervous system, feeding your brain with more nerve activity, both electrically and chemically, and having all of that neural activity connect to the physical body for its expression.

When we think of listening, we immediately think of our ears. Our ears are where we receive audible stimuli that activate the nerve endings that transmit information to our brains. This is just the beginning of a very complex journey of listening.

Listening is not limited to your ears. Your whole body listens, all the time. The nerve endings in your hands, eyes, skin and other organs all provide awareness, via communication between one nerve and the next.

When you're standing in a studio and the music begins to play, the nerve endings in your toes listen, through the vibrations and support of the floor. The body experiences an emotional connection to the music, themes, thoughts, images and environmental framework sensations. Your body's nervous system is in constant communications mode.

Think of your nervous system as a chain of links. If the first link sends a message to the second link but the second link isn't receiving (or listening), there's no way the message will get to the end of the chain. Therefore, just as your nerves are giving and receiving, we as dance storytellers have to emulate the same.

The best part about asking questions is that you don't have to have the answer up front; you just have to honestly engage in the "doing" or trying to figure out the answer. Once you make this shift, the moment becomes real to you and you now move beyond bad acting, to exploratory, discovery-based great acting! As you dance, if you ask yourself the right questions pertaining to your circumstance, you will not have to "act" because you will have the ability to "react" as you discover the answer to your questions. We'll discuss organizing your work with exploration and discovery at the helm more in chapter 5.

To reiterate, the dancer's ability to listen with their entire body is paramount to dance storytelling and acting for dancers. If you can learn to listen successfully on a three-dimensional plane (with your entire body), get excited, because you're off to a great start.

How can you apply what you've learned in Chapter 2 to increase the level in which you listen with your entire body while you dance?

_____
_____
_____
_____
_____
_____
_____
_____
_____
_____
_____
_____
_____
_____
_____
_____
_____
_____
_____
_____
_____
_____
_____
_____
_____
_____
_____

Notes: _____

_____

_____

_____

_____

_____

_____

_____

_____

_____

_____

_____

_____

_____

_____

_____

_____

_____

_____

_____

_____

_____

_____

_____

_____

_____

_____

_____

_____

_____

_____

_____

_____

_____

CHAPTER 3

LEVEL OF FUN AND COMMITMENT

If you're not having fun, you're doing something wrong! Being a dancer is a lot of hard work and should take a great deal of time and preparation, but the "doing" of dancing, acting, singing, and storytelling should be FUN.

A theatrical production is called a "play" for a reason! Art and art-making should be fun; if it's not fun for you, then you must answer for yourself: why is that? Is this honestly something you like doing? Something you really want?

Michael Jackson, one of the greatest performers, dancers, and dance storytellers of all time, is most remembered for his high commitment and level

of fun. His audiences are supercharged by his passion, commitment, and specificity, all of which are unlocked using this simple Acting for Dancers tool, the foundation of which is "you must have fun!"

Think of any great performer or dancer. Their level of fun and commitment is very high, and a key component of artistry. Because of this, they end up being great storytellers.

When you're having fun, tension naturally falls

away. The freedom in your body allows you to be open to listen; this listening without tension then allows you to respond organically which makes great acting happen!

Notice how important this simple and seemingly trivial foundation, is and how the other elements stem from here. All combined, they go on to make great artists and amazing dance storytellers.

The most interesting dance artists that surface over the course of our workshop experiences are the ones who are having the most fun. The cream of the crop are the artists who find enjoyment in listening and responding. In turn, we as the viewers are also having fun, and can easily follow their journey.

On a scale of 1 to 10, your level of fun needs to stay at a 10 at all times. When you maintain level 10 fun, you'll best be able to explore the other fundamental tools of the craft. So: in addition to the focus, concentration, relaxation, and listening with

your entire body that you've learned about, level 10 fun has to be established to unlock the door to the next level and key elements.

Do you sometimes have problems committing to your work and finding your fun place? If you do, then stop for a moment and figure out what needs to be done to catch yourself up.

The basics need to be nailed down or you will become frustrated along your journey. Making choices and taking risks in building characters will be horrifying to you. You will have issues exploring,

listening, and you won't want to practice. As a result, you won't be getting better and improving your dancing, which will only make you more irritated and discouraged. And forget about people wanting to watch you; more importantly, forget about them being willing to pay money to watch you!

If this process isn't fun for you, stop. Go find something to do that you really enjoy and want to dedicate yourself to.

Dedication is what will open the doors to improvement and mastering your art, which keeps you marching forward. It's seeing your improvement that provides the joy of accomplishment and keeps you working within the process for even more improvement.

So, let's figure that you're maintaining high levels of focus and concentration, engaging your whole body in listening, keeping your fun and commitment levels up at 10. We've got additional work to do with more elements for you to learn about!

Most people can't imagine that acting would be difficult or tiring and exhausting work. However, you now understand why IT IS! Engaging the body and mind on this level means using a muscle that's normally underused. The amount of time and research that we have spent developing new works of art is huge, years in some cases, and always comes at a great expense.

Because this work takes a great deal of energy and

mental force, it's very important to be healthy, rested, and well-nourished, so your mind and body have the fuel they need to support you and to respond properly.

Remember, without high levels of fun and commitment, you won't be prepared for the next level of artistry. Approach your work with an understanding of where you are on a scale of 1-10. Level 10 FUN and COMMITMENT will allow you to freely make choices, build character, and create circumstance, which we're excited to discuss in Chapter Four and Chapter Five.

How can you apply what you've learned in Chapter 3 to reach level 10 fun and commitment in your dancing? ———————————

———————————————————————————————
———————————————————————————————
———————————————————————————————
———————————————————————————————
———————————————————————————————
———————————————————————————————
———————————————————————————————
———————————————————————————————
———————————————————————————————
———————————————————————————————
———————————————————————————————
———————————————————————————————
———————————————————————————————
———————————————————————————————
———————————————————————————————
———————————————————————————————
———————————————————————————————
———————————————————————————————
———————————————————————————————
———————————————————————————————
———————————————————————————————
———————————————————————————————
———————————————————————————————
———————————————————————————————

Notes: _____

_____

_____

_____

_____

_____

_____

_____

_____

_____

_____

_____

_____

_____

_____

_____

_____

_____

_____

_____

_____

_____

_____

_____

_____

_____

_____

_____

_____

_____

_____

_____

_____

_____

_____

_____

_____

CHAPTER 4

IMAGINE THIS!
BUILDING CIRCUMSTANCE

Do you know any kid who doesn't enjoy playing house, office, cops and robbers, or some other video game in an imaginary world? Of course not! As children we rely on our imagination as our main source of fun and entertainment – it's our way of living!

As we get older, we're still capable of utilizing our imagination, but for whatever unfortunate reasons, most of us pack it away. We tuck it neatly up into our mental attic (or some other form of storage somewhere).

Today, we're going to unpack that puppy and put it to work! Dancing can be as stimulating as playing house, cops and robbers, cowboys and indians – or even more fun!

The great artists and dance storytellers rely on imagination as an essential and powerful tool. With our imagination we are able to transform internally, which then translates to what we do externally. We teleport from the studio to another place (an imaginary world)! Building circumstance is defining that place for you as the dancer.

Dancers who use imaginative work have the ability to better translate emotion and story to audiences.

Think about it. Take two dancers with the same technique or technical ability, give them the same choreography, and allow them both to dance or perform the piece. The performances will be completely different based on their training, their bodies, and so on. But it's certain that the dancer who applies the use of their imagination will be far more interesting and engaging to watch.

During workshop weekends, artists analyze
their peers' work during and after exploration
and element exercises. The "imaginative muscle"

workers always rise to the top of the "most interesting" list, and inevitably they are the performers we want to continue watching.

During a coaching session a few days ago, a young woman's mother came into the studio after we'd been working for a bit, and watched her daughter perform a piece that I'm sure she had seen hundreds of times before. When her daughter had finished performing the piece, the mom couldn't suppress her excitement and yelled, "I really felt it!"

What does that mean, she felt it? What happened during the run-through of the piece that particular time that hadn't happened before? Had the young dancer's dance technique gotten better in the twenty minutes that I had been working with her? No – especially since I'm not a dancer, and I wasn't coaching her dance technique.

She was using her imagination!

She was working internally, which translated through her entire body and outside to us, her audience, the viewers.

At this point, we can now fully understand why the tools we've established must be in use. To utilize the imagination, one must be relaxed, focused and concentrated, listening with the entire body, committed and having fun! This young dancer was doing all of those things.

It's important to understand that the use of circumstance-building and imagination does not have to be linear. You can be in "one place" in one moment and "another place" the next moment.

Once you know the movement well enough to do it without consciously thinking about it, you're ready to try layering in circumstance and asking questions.

Where are you? What are you doing? Who are you speaking to? Why? Why are you here and speaking/or doing what you're doing?

Let your mind loose to run free! Find the enjoyment in beginning to ask these beautiful
questions. Be careful not to limit yourself to an-
swering them directly or in some practical way,
but rather through the exploration of the physical movement.

Believing that your thoughts or circumstances
have to make practical or linear sense can allow
you to become trapped. The key is to help you,
the artist, engage and connect with the movement on an internal level. It's what you will hear
us refer to on weekends as "drop in."

What it takes to "drop in" is different for every artist, because we're all wired differently. As
you build your process, stay open to all options.
You'll learn to add tools and elements to your
own toolboxes as you go.

Some people work well envisioning colors,

or shapes, or animals, while others work better knowing where they are or whom they are
speaking to; whatever works for you is the right
thing for you!

How can you apply what you've learned in Chapter 4 to create and build circumstance while you dance? ————————————

_____

_____

_____

_____

_____

_____

_____

_____

_____

_____

_____

_____

_____

_____

_____

_____

_____

_____

_____

_____

_____

_____

_____

_____

_____

Notes: _____

_____

_____

_____

_____

_____

_____

_____

_____

_____

_____

_____

_____

_____

_____

_____

_____

_____

_____

_____

_____

_____

_____

_____

_____

_____

_____

_____

_____

_____

CHAPTER 5

DISCOVERY! INVESTIGATION AND EXPLORATION

Sir Francis Bacon, the brilliant English philosopher, statesman, scientist, lawyer, jurist, author, and pioneer of the scientific method, asserted, "If a person will begin with certainties, he will end in doubts; but if he will be content to begin with doubts, he will end in certainties." What this means is, it's important to investigate, ask questions, explore!

As you build your process with the use of circumstance, it's very important to also understand the need for exploration and discovery.

Over workshop weekends we discuss the very important element of the unknown. We pretty much always want to err on the side of not knowing as we make choices and build our dance work. Why is that?

You can think of it as similar to going to the movies. No one likes a movie that's predictable – why watch it if you know right from the beginning how it's going to end! It holds your interest as you see how the story unfolds, and enjoyable as you watch the players discover what they don't already know.

It's the same on our journey in acting for dancers. We want to remain in the place of the unknown, discovering in every moment with and through the choreographed or given movement.

Great acting is a discovery process; by asking the right questions once you've entered into the world you've created, you'll be given the ability to discover and find things, in what we refer to as "moments."

As you work through the dance movement: investigate, and discover what you are or could be doing.

Moments can change, so stay open to all the possibilities. Once you've found something that feels right and connects the outside movement with the internal inspiration, keep it! In addition, each time you work, try to find more depth in the moments you have, and discover new ones!

Working in this way makes dancing very fun and keeps it new and fresh. You'll find yourself free from outside distractions and you won't worry about technical issues in the same way as before.

The more work you do to be specific about where you are and what you're doing, the more fun you'll have discovering moments during your journey.

The dancers participating in the workshop weekends who have built clear circumstance for themselves find it much easier to do the investigation and discovery.

Do the work to build all the aspects of your environment. For example, if you're in the forest, be specific about what kind of forest and what you see, what you hear, what the ground feels like under your feet. Or perhaps you're under water, or in the dessert – and maybe it's Jell-O; whatever it is, be specific and define all the details!

The more energy you use to you apply yourself here, the deeper and more authentic your imaginative discovery and investigative work will be.

You'll use all these findings and discoveries to execute your dance over and over again in an organic and fresh way, with the same connection. Remember, if you work in the theatre, you are live and you have to repeat your performance night after night. A critical challenge for you is that it has to seem to the audience you're experiencing each moment for the very first time. However, you and I know (and the audience knows, too) that you're not experiencing the moment for the first time, because you've performed this piece or show dozens of times, and if you're at a professional level, you may have been performing the same piece for many years!

The important question is, then, how do you keep the performance and its moments fresh every night for the new onlookers and audience members?

We established back in Chapters One and Two that the actors we all love the best are the ones who are the most believable and authentic in each moment, and this is what you're working now to achieve.

The more you discover and search, the more interesting you are as a performer and artist; audience members care when you care, feel when you feel, and thrill when you discover.

Dancers in our workshop weekends who investigate and discover in their work are the most interesting to watch, and become elevated by their peers as "the best."

This recognition isn't specifically or solely because of their technical skill and ability, but because of their dance storytelling; the development of their imagination, focus, circumstance, listening, heightened awareness, investigation, and discovery.

How can you apply what you've learned in Chapter 5 to increase your level of discovery, investigation, and exploration in your dance?

_____

_____
_____
_____
_____
_____
_____
_____
_____
_____
_____
_____
_____
_____
_____
_____
_____
_____
_____
_____
_____
_____
_____
_____
_____

Notes: _____

_____

_____

_____

_____

_____

_____

_____

_____

_____

_____

_____

_____

_____

_____

_____

_____

_____

_____

_____

_____

_____

_____

_____

_____

_____

_____

_____

CHAPTER 6

CHARACTER BUILDING

Even though every dance work is different, our development process should remain the same. The particular tools that we choose to include in our process vary depending on the piece of work and what's needed for us to connect internally, or as we say, drop in.

Character building is different from circumstance building in that it's specific to defining and detailing "who" you are. In character building, we're asking specific questions to uncover your background, or what we call "backstory."

This tool is not needed for every dance piece, but it's important that you develop this skill because at times, it will come in very handy.

If you have the ability to drop in while using another element like circumstance, place, texture, feel, or color, you may not require any character work, but there are going to be some pieces which are harder for you, as the artist, to connect with and the use of character building might help you a lot.

Earlier we said that these elements of acting are employed to help you connect to the work or internalize the movement so that it reflects on the outside. If you are having trouble dropping in and nothing else is working, explore with character building.

As in circumstance building, the more detailed work you do, the better. Some of the questions you might pose are: Who are you? How old are you? Where are you from? or Where did you grow up? Why are you here and why are you doing what you're doing?

Trying to answer these questions will require you to begin building story elements. Again, we repeat, this story does not have to be linear or make practical sense. If you are a wizard in one moment, you could still be a clown or a frog in the next; it all depends on the movement and what you need in order to find connection, purpose, and internalized intention.

Asking these questions permits you to have the foundation of information and circumstance you need for your imagination to take you deeper in your discovery of what purpose the movement has and plays into the story – and that's exciting and fun. Sometimes dancers think that the reason for asking the questions is so that you can go into the dance piece "knowing" everything – clearly, that's not what we mean at all.

Dancers' instruments are so special because of how responsive they are. Actors express the majority of their story with words, while dancers do it with movement.

In Acting for Dancers, we build understanding of a character to the point where we dance the movement so that it corresponds to the (unspoken) words of the character.

In order to do this, you must have the foundation and understanding of the character you can get from preparing the background. The more work you do in preparation, the more full and specific you're dancing will become.

A notebook is a great aid here, and if you don't have one, get one! We always ask dancers to bring notebooks for completing this kind of work, as well as taking notes throughout the workshop weekend.

You'll be amazed at how working with a journal on character building will enhance your in-studio work and understanding; sparking your imagination in ways you'd never dream of, along with enhancing your ability to dance with purpose and tell a story.

Building characters is fun!

Yes, it's intense, and it takes a lot of focus, concentration, and commitment, but the reward is great as your smart and special instrument responds to the new stimulus and information.

How can you apply what you've learned in Chapter 6 to create and build a specific character in your dance? —————————————

——————————————————————————
——————————————————————————
——————————————————————————
——————————————————————————
——————————————————————————
——————————————————————————
——————————————————————————
——————————————————————————
——————————————————————————
——————————————————————————
——————————————————————————
——————————————————————————
——————————————————————————
——————————————————————————
——————————————————————————
——————————————————————————
——————————————————————————
——————————————————————————
——————————————————————————
——————————————————————————
——————————————————————————
——————————————————————————
——————————————————————————
——————————————————————————
——————————————————————————
——————————————————————————
——————————————————————————
——————————————————————————
——————————————————————————

Notes: _____

_____

_____

_____

_____

_____

_____

_____

_____

_____

_____

_____

_____

_____

_____

_____

_____

_____

_____

_____

_____

_____

_____

_____

_____

_____

_____

_____

_____

_____

CHAPTER 7

STORYTELLING

What is the story you'd like to tell?

One of the most beautiful things about creating art is that it requires each of us artists to tell our

own special story. As a dancer you must bring yourself to all the work you do. Developing your voice is exhilarating; you can express things in a way that's unique and only available to you!

Everyone is different, of course, and that makes life interesting. We each have different perspectives and the world wants to hear your story, through your perspective, in your voice.

Dancing is more fun (and your audience will get more out of it) when your imagination is engaged, when you feel connected to a story, purpose or circumstance. When you've rehearsed and learned the movement well enough to let it all go and just dance, that's when your performance will shine! Your insecurities about the moves, your body, what viewers are thinking, will all fall away as you explore a character. Be bold and take a journey, while utilizing your own amazing imagination.

A great story has a clear beginning, middle,

and end. So as you build your circumstance and character, plot the arc of your story thoughtfully. Do begin with a clear starting point. Once you understand where to begin, jump to the end: what is different? At the end, how have you changed? How have you grown, and what have you learned?

To figure out the middle, walk through the steps of organically getting from your starting point to your ending. Does it make sense? Is the journey believable? It is? Good, then that's your middle.

Here's a caution that bears repeating: Don't get trapped in linear thinking. When building story elements and arc, you should be connected to the work, so feel free to create a story arc that serves your circumstance and character. But remember to stay open; your story arc does not have to be entirely logical.

The depth of your dance at this point in the process should be full, with numerous layers. Every part of the movement choreography should be specific and purposeful. The movement should now not only be technically correct, but also evoke an emotional response from your audience.

Many people come to the theatre because they want and expect to be emotionally moved, and to get swept up into someone else's reality for a short while as a release from their own lives. Your ability to successfully complete this task will make you a sought-after "dance storyteller."

It's worth mentioning Michael Jackson again here. He was not only the King of Pop but he was also the King of Storytelling. Go back and listen to his music. All of his songs have a very clear beginning, middle, and end, making it easy for his audience to connect emotionally and identify practically.

I hope you're excited for the next phase of your dancing abilities, because you now have the theory and tools to begin your very special journey as a storyteller!

How can you apply what you've learned in Chapter 7 about storytelling to your dance?

Notes: _____

_____

_____

_____

_____

_____

_____

_____

_____

_____

_____

_____

_____

_____

_____

_____

_____

_____

_____

_____

_____

_____

_____

_____

_____

_____

_____

_____

CHAPTER 8

NOW TO THE DANCING!

Okay, so now you can forget everything and go dance!

The creative process is never-ending, and as we reach to become more skilled within our craft, we continue to realize that we will always be learning and developing.

It's okay! Perfect practice only makes "almost perfect."

We truly hope this book inspires you in your journey to becoming a great dancer yourself, or to helping other dancers become great storytellers.

Now to dancing!

To dance is to reach for a word that doesn't exist,
To sing the heartsong of a thousand generations,
To feel the meaning of a moment in time.

– Beth Jones

Dancing is just discovery, discovery, discovery.

- Martha Graham

How can we know the dancer from the dance?

– William Butler Yeats

The truest expression of a people is in its dance
and in its music. Bodies never lie.

– Agnes de Mille

Dancers are instruments,
like a piano the choreographer plays.

- George Balanchine

Ballet is not technique but a way of expression
that comes more closely to
the inner language of man than any other.

– *George Borodin*

Great dancers are not great because of their
technique, they are great because of their passion.

– Martha Graham

CHAPTER 9

ARTISTS AT WORK

"Thank you guys so much for an amazing weekend! I really appreciate the time that you took to make me a better dancer and to really feel what dancing is all about. I got one of the most greatest tips from J... Level 10 fun, Level 10 commitment. This was the BEST experience I've had in this crazy, amazing dance world. To be honest my mom said this workshop was actually worth paying for! I love all of you so much!"

— *Brooklyn #AFDAlumni*

"My daughter had the opportunity to attend the workshop in Seattle last weekend and I just wanted to say: THANK YOU! As I have been telling everybody (seriously…everybody), it was such a welcome respite from the competition circuit. To be able to free herself from competing and comparing herself to others, and truly enjoy bonding, creating and the art of dance itself was so needed, so rejuvenating. My daughter feels refreshed and reconnected with why she began dancing in the first place! She has been inspired! Have you ever considered twice-yearly work-shops here? Quarterly?"

– Rochelle, Seattle | ParentsOnAFD

...

"Sadie loves the AFD workshop and has at-tended the past two years in Vancouver. AFD gives dancers a safe place to focus on express-ing themselves. It is not the typical convention/workshop atmosphere, where auditions are held, and competition is part of the learning process.

Because of that, I feel like she learns that much more—she is free to simply concentrate on what is being taught and what she is moved to do. She can focus on what the dance means to HER and what SHE is trying to portray, not what she thinks the instructors are looking for. And, speaking of instructors, they are all top-notch. Every instructor is supportive and nurturing, while challenging each dancer to find their best and authentic selves. Between them all, there is a wonderful balance of technique instruction as well as creative exploration. There is not another workshop I've found with this atmosphere and focus. I'm happy to see a Seattle date!"

– Jill, Vancouver | ParentsOnAFD

...

"My daughter Olivia was at this amazing workshop for the first time. She learned so much in two short days. She left with a new-found confidence and J. Alex made her feel extra special in her solo coaching, teaching her ways to believe in herself. What amazing faculty you have, making us all feel welcome, from the parents to the dancers. I hope to bring her to another event in the near future."

— Kristin, Seattle | ParentsOnAFD

...

"What an INCREDIBLE weekend! My daughter learned so much this weekend at Acting for Dancers. As a parent, I loved that the focus was more on the dance itself as an art form and not on the amount of 'tricks' you can do. So much creative expression and movement. GREAT JOB... Hope you are back soon! Thank you for bringing this LOVE of dance and expression!"

— Heather, Phoenix | ParentsOnAFD

...

"My experience with Acting for Dancers taught me that the reaction of a story not only should be portrayed through my face but also throughout my body expression and most importantly my heart. It made me really take in a story, apply it to a situation I can relate to, and visually see it through my eyes while dancing. Now when I dance I get chills and feel like I am in the situation. Dancing has never felt so real and my movement has never looked so true. Can't wait to learn from them again this summer!"

— *Addison, Phoenix | AFDAlumni*

...

"Acting For Dancers and Sarah Brinson, I cannot thank you enough for this weekend and giving my three girls the chance to work with you again. They all are so moved and inspired by you and J Brinson, the quality of work you produce, and transmit to the dancers is very admirable and I truly think you are an amazing teacher & mentor to all!! What you did for Bella today, so appreciate the words of wisdom and your advice, she truly needed to hear that from you both, so wanted to say thank you again for acknowledging and helping her feel that she is going somewhere with her dancing, and did tons for her confidence Also with Alyssa. J is spectacular at what he does and the two of you make the most amazing dynamic duo, it's so inspiring and valued by a parent that you take the time to do these workshops and the one-on-ones with them. They all take away so much more than dancing, so again lovely to see you and J and your wonderful friendly team. Love you, take care, and all the best at your next workshop!!!!"

— *Gianna, Bella, Sofia and Alyssa*
AFD Alumni | ParentsOnAFD

...

"What an inspiring weekend for our kids! Thanks so much for taking the time to share your amazing talents with all of them. Jordan took so much away from this weekend and wants to attend more classes! See you at an AFD in the future!"

— *Jamie, Seattle | ParentsOnAFD*

"My favorite part of AFD was learning how to incorporate aspects from our acting exercises into our dancing. Little things that J taught us had a surprisingly huge impact on our dancing, which was an incredible experience. I feel as if I am a completely new dancer after this workshop, and I learned how to express things through my body and my dancing I had never before been able to do."

— *Mekayla, Atlanta | AFD Alumni*

...

"My daughter, Aislynn, thoroughly enjoyed the AFD Workshop! She felt that she learned so much more in two days than she has at any other workshop or convention that she has attended. We hope to be able to attend another workshop soon! Thank you Sarah, J. Alex and your other faculty for an amazing and unforgettable weekend!"

— *Leighann, Seattle | ParentsOnAFD*

"Thank you all so much for this amazing experience. Kailey enjoyed it tremendously. She came away feeling inspired and believing in herself. The girls loved that they learned a new side, of dance and how to express themselves and just not dance combos like most conventions. It made me proud to see them excited to learn and share. Thank you again, and hope Kailey can attend another AFD!!!"

— Tami, Seattle | ParentsOnAFD

...

"This was an amazing experience for my daughter Olivia. I just can't say enough how wonderful this was. I hope to see you all again."

— Kristen, Seattle | ParentsOnAFD

...

"Acting for Dancers taught me to listen to the words and the sounds in music and to share stories and ideas through dance. I learned to use my face and my entire body to tell a story. In fact, at a recent dance competition, I won a judges award for being a 'super storyteller.' I know that it is because of what I learned from Sarah, J. Alex and the other AFD instructors. Acting for Dancers is my very favorite workshop. It is really fun and such a positive and upbeat experience. I left feeling like I can do anything I put my mind to. I can't wait to go back!"

— *Kaya | AFDAlumni*

...

"I loved my time at Acting for Dancers. Their staff has changed my life. AFD created a safe and loving environment where I felt that I could get out of my comfort zone and be free. They've helped me grow as a dancer and as a person. They taught me to trust and believe in myself and have it 'shine' through in my dancing. I can't wait for the next workshop. xo"

— *Isabella, Orem | AFDAlumni*

"Thank you #ActingForDancers! Because of this weekend with Sarah Brinson and J Alex Brinson I'm a TOTALLY new dancer!"

— *Zoe, Orem | AFDAlumni*

BE INSPIRED.

Notes: _____

_____

_____

_____

_____

_____

_____

_____

_____

_____

_____

_____

_____

_____

_____

_____

_____

_____

_____

_____

_____

_____

_____

_____

_____

_____

_____

_____

Notes: _____

_____
_____
_____
_____
_____
_____
_____
_____
_____
_____
_____
_____
_____
_____
_____
_____
_____
_____
_____
_____
_____
_____
_____
_____
_____
_____
_____
_____
_____

ACTING FOR DANCERS

WWW.ACTINGFORDANCERSWORKSHOP.COM

 ACTING FOR DANCERS WORKSHOP   @ACTING4DANCERS ACTINGFORDANCERS